BAYERN PANORAMA

GEORG KÜRZINGER

BAYERN PANORAMA

EDITION BRAUS

Das ewige Leben

Wenn im Himmel wirklich Menschen wohnen, dann kann es gut sein, dass deren Kinder das gleiche Spiel spielen wie wir, als wir noch Kinder waren. Wir legten uns in eine frische Sommerwiese, verschränkten die Arme hinter unseren Nacken und blickten in den Himmel. In den Wolkenformen suchten wir die Ebenbilder unseres Alltags: Ein Baum. Ein Fußball. Das Auto unseres Vaters. Die Nase des Nachbarn.

Bei den Kindern im Weltall funktioniert das Spiel wahrscheinlich genauso, nur andersrum. Sie sitzen auf den Wolken und blicken hinab auf die Erde. Sie sehen sich die Kontinente und die Länder an, die Meere und die Seen. Und sie suchen nach Formen und Figuren: Der Verlauf der Donau gleicht dem sinkenden Aktienkurs einer Bank und Österreich sieht aus wie ein Wiener Schnitzel.

Bayern hingegen sieht vom Himmel aus betrachtet irgendwie langweilig aus. Keine Raute, keine Breze, kein Audi, noch nicht einmal ein BMW. Mit viel Phantasie könnte man in der Gestalt des Landes vielleicht allenfalls einen sehr gebeugten Löwen ohne Schwanz und Füße erkennen. Dabei allerdings müsste das krumme Eck in der Höhe von Würzburg als Kopf herhalten, was schon allein deshalb nicht geht, weil sich dann in der Gegend von Passau der Hintern des Tieres befände. Einen solchen Vergleich hätte selbst Passau nicht verdient.

Belassen wir es also bei der eher langweiligen Interpretation, nämlich dass der Freistaat Bayern vom Himmel aus gesehen einem etwas ausgefransten Rechteck ähnelt: Die südliche Grenze zieht eine Linie vom Bodensee links unten bis rechts hinüber an die tschechische Grenze; von dort senkrecht nach Norden bis tief hinein ins Fichtelgebirge; dann wieder links Richtung Westen bis nach Aschaffenburg, das sich tief ins hessische Land beugt; und schließlich wieder runter, zurück nach Lindau am Bodensee, wo das Leben soviel wärmer und leichter zu sein scheint als hoch im Norden in der kargen Oberpfalz. Das alles ist Bayern, und bis auf ein paar Beulen und Buchten in der geografischen Anmutung des Landes handelt es sich dabei um ein doch ziemlich kompaktes Stück Erde.

Rein äußerlich mag dieser Eindruck stimmen. Die Wälder und Wiesen sind im Sommer durchweg satt und grün, und auch die übrigen Jahreszeiten haben das Land und seine Menschen so fest im Griff wie früher nur der Dorfpfarrer. Über all dem wölbt sich ein weiß-blau geschecktes Himmelszelt und oftmals scheint es, als stamme dieses nachgerade unwirkliche Bayern aus einem Bilderbuch, das andernorts verteilt wird, um den Menschen dort zu zeigen, dass es sich doch lohnt, an die Existenz des Paradieses und des ewigen Lebens zu glauben.

In Wirklichkeit jedoch ist das bayerische Leben noch immer so organisiert wie seit Ewigkeiten: Widersprüchlich und getrieben vom eifersüchtigen Ehrgeiz der drei konkurrierenden Stämme aus Altbayern, Schwaben und Franken. Während aber die Mehrheit der Deutschen ihre Geschichte als eine Folge von Brüchen und Teilungen begreift, konnten die Bayern seit dem 9. Jahrhundert, mehr oder weniger, ihre territoriale Einheit bewahren.

Vor allem deshalb verstehen sich die Bayern als anders. Anders als die anderen. Und wäre Deutschland nach dem Krieg einst nicht in Ost und West, sondern in Nord und Süd zerteilt worden – niemand kann sich heute sicher sein, ob diese beiden Hälften jemals wieder zusammengefunden hätten.

Heute jedenfalls ist Bayern ein bisschen wie ein kleines Frankreich. Mit einem bisweilen penetranten Sinn für geschichtliche Kontinuität und einem aus fränkischer Sicht nicht minder penetranten Zentralismus, in dem die hauptstädtische Elite den Ton angibt und der Rest des Landes zu parieren hat. Die Ministerialbürokratie in ihren Regierungspalästen entlang der Münchner Isar verwandelte über Jahrzehnte hinweg ein armes Bauernland in ein wohlhabendes Gewerbegebiet namens Freistaat. Der ästhetische Preis, den das Land dabei für seinen wirtschaftlichen Aufstieg zu zahlen hat, ist hoch, vor allem abseits der Touristenrouten, an den Rändern der Dörfer und Gemeinden, wo oft bunte Baumärkte in den Himmel ragen und mannshohe Plastikkühe ein bisschen Heimatgefühl vermitteln sollen.

Dennoch erscheint das Bajuwarische bei alledem so unverwüstlich wie die *France profonde*, und gerade weil die Einheimischen so sehr danach streben, für alle anderen erkennbar tief in sich verwurzelt zu sein, sehnen sie sich ab und an auch nach Höherem: Dann investieren sie in die Forschung und in die Zukunft. Die Franzosen sagen dazu *les grands projet*s, die Bayern *Laptop und Lederhose*. So grotesk jedem Außenstehenden dieser Dualismus von Vergangenheit und Zukunft erscheinen mag, so sehr bildet er doch das Fundament der Identität des modernen Durchschnittsbayern.

Fürwahr bizarr, aber das hierzulande gültige Credo *Leben und leben lassen* gilt eben nicht mehr nur für Laubfrösche, sondern auch für Weltanschauungen.

Nur manchmal, ganz selten, gerät das System ein wenig ins Stocken. Wenn zum Beispiel ein Transrapid nicht gebaut wird, eine Landesbank vor dem Ruin steht, ein Fußballverein am Saisonende ausnahmsweise einmal nicht Erster ist, der Rest der Republik gehässig über den bayerischen Papst herzieht und das Volk seiner Volkspartei auch noch die absolute Mehrheit verweigert. Gewiss, ja, ein *annus horribilis*, aber alle wissen: Auch das geht vorüber wie der in den Köpfen der Bayern dröhnende Föhn eines Sommertages.

Solange über der Oberpfalz morgens noch die Sonne aufgeht und sie abends im Bodensee wieder versinkt, geht das ewige bayerische Leben weiter. Und eines darf man dabei nicht vergessen: Vom Himmel aus gesehen fließen Bayerns Flüsse immer aufwärts.

DOMINIK WICHMANN

Dr. Dominik Wichmann, geboren 1971 in München. Seit dem Jahr 2000 Chefredakteur des Magazins der Süddeutschen Zeitung.

Eternal Immutable Life

If there really are people living in heaven, it may well be that their children play the same sort of games as we did when we were children. We lay down in a lush summer meadow with our arms behind our heads and looked up at the sky. In the cloud formations, we tried to find likenesses of everyday things around us: a tree, a ball, the family car, our neighbor's nose.

For children who live in outer space, the game probably works the same way, only the other way round. They sit on clouds and peer down toward the Earth. They look at the continents and landmasses, the oceans and lakes. And they also try to find familiar shapes and figures – the course of the Danube might resemble the falling prices of bank shares, while Austria looks like a Wiener schnitzel.

Seen from the sky, Bavaria looks rather unspectacular, though. Not diamond- or pretzel-shaped, not like an Audi or even a BMW. With a lot of fantasy, the shape of this German state might distantly call to mind a lion bent over virtually double and lacking a tail or feet. If so, the crooked end up by Würzburg would have to do service as the head; but that won't work, if for no other reason than because the region around Passau would then have to be the animal's rear end. And even Passau doesn't deserve that sort of analogy.

So, let's stick to the somewhat mundane interpretation, i.e., that the Free State of Bavaria seen from the air resembles a rather battered and frayed rectangle. Its southern border is a line extending from Lake Constance at the bottom left to the Czech border on the right; from here, it runs vertically northward, cutting deep into the hilly Fichtelgebirge region, before again turning left and westward as far as Aschaffenburg, which pokes some way into the state of Hesse; now, it proceeds south back to Lindau on Lake Constance, where life seems so much more balmy and carefree than up north in the craggy Upper Palatinate. All this is what we call Bavaria, and apart from a few bumps and dents in its geographic outline, it really is a compact chunk of land.

In purely physical terms, this impression might be correct. During the summer, the forests and fields are lush and green wherever you look, and the other seasons have the whole state and its inhabitants no less tightly under control than the village priest used to. The sky that arches over the countryside is everywhere the same mixture of blue with white flecks, and it often seems as though this almost unreal Bavaria might have popped out of some picture-book that is passed around in other places to show people there that it is, after all, a good thing to believe in the existence of paradise and eternal life.

In actual fact, though, Bavarian life is still organized just as it has been for untold ages: full of contradictions and driven along by the jealous ambitions of the three competing ancestral lineages from 'Old' Bavaria, Swabia and Franconia. Yet, whereas the majority of Germans regard their history as a sequence of fractures and splits, the Bavarians have been able, more or less, to retain the integrity of their territory since the 9th century.

It is for this reason above all else that the Bavarians regard themselves as different. Different to others. And if, after the war, Germany had been divided not into East and West but into North and South, no-one would now be able to claim with any certainty that the two halves would ever have become reunited again.

Nowadays, at any rate, Bavaria is rather like a small version of France: sometimes manifesting an irksome insistence on its historical continuity and, from the Franconian point of view, a no less irksome tendency toward centralism, with the elite of its capital calling the tune and everyone else doing their best to fight their own corner. Over a period lasting several decades, the ministerial bureaucracy housed in governmental palaces along the River Isar in Munich has succeeded in transforming a penurious state of farmers into a prosperous economic region boasting the title, 'Free State.' In terms of outward appearance, the price it has had to pay for such commercial aggrandizement has been high indeed, especially off the tourist track. Thus, on the outskirts of villages and towns, where glaringly colored home-improvement stores rear up skyward, the odd life-size plastic cow is meant to add a homely rustic touch.

Nonetheless, the Bavarian character seems to be as indestructible as *France profonde*. Actually, it's precisely because the locals try so hard to convey to others the impression of being so firmly rooted in their own traditions that they do, now and again, set their sights on loftier goals – and that's when they invest in research and in the future. The French call this *les grands projets*; for Bavarians, it's a matter of *Laptop und Lederhose*. As peculiar as this dualism between past and present may appear to outsiders, this is, in fact, the very bedrock of the average modern Bavarian's sense of identity. Bizarre it might be, but the generally held motto, 'live and let live,' no longer applies just to the birds and the bees but to a whole way of looking at the world we live in.

Just occasionally, very rarely, the system shows signs of faltering. Such as when the high-speed Transrapid train link was abandoned, when the state bank was on the edge of collapse, or when, for once, a certain soccer club does not win the national league. Or when the rest of the country has nasty things to say about the Bavarian Pope, and the Bavarian voters don't give their own political party a clear election majority. An *annus horribilis* for sure, but as everyone is well aware, all of this will also have an end, just like the southerly wind, the foehn, that gusts over the heads of Bavarians on certain summer days.

As long as the sun rises above the Upper Palatinate in the morning and sinks again into Lake Constance at night, immutable Bavarian life will go on as before. And there's one other thing we should always bear in mind: seen from the sky, Bavaria's rivers always appear to flow upward.

DOMINIK WICHMANN

Dr. Dominik Wichmann was born in Munich in 1971. Since 2000, he has been editor-in-chief of the Süddeutsche Zeitung Magazine.

München, Marienplatz und Frauenkirche
View over Marienplatz toward the New City Hall and Church of Our Lady in Munich

10 | Brunnenhof der Residenz in München
The Fountain Courtyard of the Residence in Munich

Maximilianeum in München, Sitz des Bayerischen Landtags
The Maximilianeum in Munich, seat of the Bavarian State Parliament

Am Eisbach im Englischen Garten, München
On the banks of the Eisbach in the English Garden, Munich

Blick auf den Monopteros im Englischen Garten, München
View toward the Monopteros in the English Garden, Munich

Schloss Nymphenburg und Schlosspark in München
Nymphenburg Castle and the Castle Garden in Munich

Amalienburg in München, Blick in das Jagdzimmer und den Spiegelsaal
The Amalienburg in Munich, view of the 'Hunting Salon' and 'Hall of Mirrors'

Einzug der Wiesnwirte auf dem Münchner Oktoberfest
Entry Procession of the Publicans at the Munich Oktoberfest

Bierzelt auf dem Oktoberfest in München
Beer tent at the Oktoberfest in Munich

Blick auf das Jüdische Zentrum Jakobsplatz mit Jüdischem Museum, neuer Hauptsynagoge und Münchner Stadtmuseum
View of the Jewish Center on Jakobsplatz, with the Jewish Museum, the new Central Synagogue and the Munich City Museum

Münchner Königsplatz mit Glyptothek und Propyläen
Königsplatz in Munich, with the Glyptothek and the Propyläen

Neues Schloss in Schleißheim bei München
The 'New Castle' in Schleissheim near Munich

Baselitz-Saal in der Pinakothek der Moderne, München
The Baselitz Room in the Pinakothek der Moderne, Munich

Blick auf Albrecht Dürers „Vier Apostel" in der Alten Pinakothek, München
View toward Albrecht Dürer's Four Apostles in the Alte Pinakothek in Munich

BMW Welt und BMW Vierzylinder, München
BMW World and BMW's 'four-cylinder' headquarters in Munich

Allianz Arena, München
The Allianz Arena, Munich

Altstadt von Landshut
Landshut's historic center

Historische Landshuter Hochzeit
The 'Landshut Wedding,' a traditional pageant

Donau und Klenzepark mit der Festungsanlage Reduit Tilly in Ingolstadt
The Danube and Klenze Park with the Reduit Tilly fortifications in Ingolstadt

Ingolstadt, Bayerisches Armeemuseum im Neuen Schloss
Ingolstadt, the Bavarian Army Museum in the New Castle

Kapellplatz in Altötting
Kapellplatz in Altötting

Freisinger Domberg
The Domberg ('Cathedral Hill') in Freising

Hallertau („Holledau"), Hopfenanbaugebiet nahe Pfaffenhofen an der Ilm
The Hallertau (or 'Holledau'), a hop-growing region near Pfaffenhofen on the River Ilm

Essing an der Altmühl
Essing on the River Altmühl

Weiden in der Oberpfalz
Weiden in the Upper Palatinate (Oberpfalz)

Die Herzogsburg in Dingolfing, heute Industriemuseum
The Herzogsburg ('Ducal Castle') in Dingolfing now houses an Industrial Museum

Wegkreuz nahe Regen
Wayside cross near Regen

Kloster Weltenburg an der Donau
Weltenburg Abbey on the Danube

Blick auf Kallmünz mit Steinerner Brücke und Burgruine
View of Kallmünz with its historic Stone Bridge and ruined fortress

Stiftsbibliothek Waldsassen in der Zisterzienser-Abtei
Waldsassen Collegiate Library in the Cistercian Abbey

Blick auf den Dom und die Steinerne Brücke in Regensburg
View toward the Cathedral and the ancient Stone Bridge in Regensburg

Der Haidplatz in Regensburg mit dem Thon-Dittmer-Palais und der Patrizierburg „Goldenes Kreuz"
Haidplatz in Regensburg with the Thon-Dittmer Palais and the 'Golden Cross' noble's palace

Blick von der Steinernen Brücke nach Regensburg
View of Regensburg from the Stone Bridge

Innenraum der Befreiungshalle in Kelheim
Interior of the Hall of Liberation (*Befreiungshalle*) above Kelheim

Blick auf das Dreiflüsseeck, den Zusammenfluss von Ilz, Donau und Inn, in Passau
View over the 'Three Rivers Elbow,' the confluence of the Ilz, Danube and Inn in Passau

Der Inn in Passau
The River Inn in Passau

Auf dem Rachel-Gipfel im Nationalpark Bayerischer Wald
The peak of Rachel Hill in the Bavarian Forest National Park

Blick von Lusen-Gipfel im Nationalpark Bayerischer Wald
View from the peak of Lusen Hill in the Bavarian Forest National Park

Tüchersfeld in der Fränkischen Schweiz
Tüchersfeld in so-called 'Franconian Switzerland'

Das „Walberla“, Zeugenberg nahe Forchheim in der Fränkischen Schweiz
The ‘Walberla,’ a butte near Forchheim in ‘Franconian Switzerland’

Nürnberg mit Blick auf die Burg
Nuremberg, view toward the Imperial Castle

Der Nürnberger Christkindlesmarkt
Nuremberg's Christmas Market, the *Christkindlesmarkt*

Die Eremitage in Bayreuth
The Hermitage in Bayreuth

Das Bayreuther Festspielhaus
The Festpielhaus, Bayreuth's opera house

Blick über Bamberg
Panoramic view of Bamberg

Im Bamberger Dom
Inside Bamberg Cathedral

Blick auf den Dom und die Alte Hofhaltung
Bamberg Cathedral and the Old Archbishop's Palace

Aussicht von der Vogelsburg auf den Main
View from the Vogelsburg toward the River Main

Blick von der Alten Mainbrücke auf die Festung Marienberg in Würzburg
View from the Old Main Bridge toward the Marienberg Fortress in Würzburg

Würzburger Residenz und Ehrenhof
Würzburg's Residence with its monumental forecourt

Würzburger Residenz und Hofgarten
Würzburg's Residence and Castle Garden

Blick vom Rathausturm auf Rothenburg ob der Tauber
View from the tower of the Old City Hall over Rothenburg ob der Tauber

St. Georgsbrunnen in Rothenburg ob der Tauber
The St.George Fountain in Rothenburg ob der Tauber

Blick vom „Daniel“, dem Kirchturm der St.-Georgs-Kirche, auf Nördlingen
View from the 'Daniel,' the tower of the Church of St. George in Nördlingen

Marktplatz und Rathaus in Memmingen
The Market Square and City Hall in Memmingen

Innenraum der Klosterkirche Ottobeuren
Interior of the Abbey Church of Ottobeuren

Blick auf die Klosterkirche Ottobeuren
View of the Abbey Church of Ottobeuren

Der Goldene Saal im Augsburger Rathaus
The Golden Hall in Augsburg's City Hall

Hafen mit Mangturm und Bayerischem Löwen in Lindau
The harbor in Lindau with its tower, the Mangturm, and the Bavarian lion

BSB

Bad Hindelang im Allgäu
Bad Hindelang in the Allgäu

Die Siplinger Nadeln im Allgäu
The so-called 'Siplinger Needles' in the Allgäu region

Blick auf Schloss Neuschwanstein
View of Neuschwanstein Castle

Schloss Neuschwanstein im Winter
Neuschwanstein Castle in the winter

Aussicht auf Schloss Hohenschwangau mit Alpsee (links) und Schwansee (rechts)
View over Hohenschwangau Castle with the Alpsee (left) and Schwansee (right) lakes

Schloss Linderhof mit Schlosspark
Linderhof Castle with its garden

Blick auf Burghausen und die Salzach
View toward Burghausen on the River Salzach

Seepromenade in Starnberg
Lakeside promenade in Starnberg

Starnberger See bei Ammerland
Lake Starnberg near Ammerland

Der Ammersee bei Herrsching
The Ammersee lake near Herrsching

Der Ammersee bei Herrsching
The Ammersee lake near Herrsching

Sachrang bei Aschau im Chiemgau
Sachrang near Aschau in the Chiemgau region

Blick in den Chiemgau bei Prien
Chiemgau landscape near Prien

Aussicht von der Kampenwand auf den Chiemsee
View toward the Chiemsee lake from the Kampenwand

Die Fraueninsel im Chiemsee
The Fraueninsel, an island on the Chiemsee

Der Chiemsee bei Chieming
The Chiemsee near Chieming

In Jenhausen nahe Weilheim
In Jenhausen near Weilheim

Am Irschenberg
By Irschenberg

104 | Landschaft bei Wolfratshausen
Landscape near Wolfratshausen

Trachtenfest in Bayrischzell
Festival of traditional costumes in Bayrischzell

Leonhardifahrt in Breitbrunn am Chiemsee
St. Leonhard's Procession in Breitbrunn by the Chiemsee

Blick auf die Wieskirche, eine Wallfahrtskirche bei Steingaden
View of the Wieskirche, a pilgrimage church near Steingaden

Innenraum der Wieskirche
Interior of the Wieskirche

Riedersteinkapelle am Tegernsee
The Riederstein Chapel on Lake Tegernsee

Dorf Schliersee am Schliersee
The village of Schliersee on the lake of the same name

Aussicht auf Wasserburg am Inn
Wasserburg on the River Inn

INNSCHIFFAHRT

Mit Lüftlmalerei gestaltete Häuser in Oberammergau
Houses decorated with frescoes (so-called *Lüftlmalerei*) in Oberammergau

„Husarenhaus“ in Garmisch-Partenkirchen
The ‘Hussars’ House’ in Garmisch-Partenkirchen

„Heumandln“ bei Mittenwald
'Haystack men' near Mittenwald

Häuser mit Lüftlmalerei in Mittenwald
Houses decorated with *Lüftlmalerei* frescoes in Mittenwald

Winterimpression bei Seebruck am Chiemsee
Winter scenery near Seebruck on the Chiemsee

Verschneite Landschaft nahe Murnau
Snow-covered landscape near Murnau

In der Partnachklamm bei Garmisch-Partenkirchen
In the Partnachklamm near Garmisch-Partenkirchen

Kuhflucht-Wasserfälle bei Farchant/ Garmisch-Partenkirchen
The Kuhflucht waterfalls near Farchant/Garmisch-Partenkirchen

Aussicht auf den Watzmann und den Königssee im Nationalpark Berchtesgaden
View toward the Watzmann peak and the Königsee lake in the Berchtesgarten National Park

Die Wallfahrtskapelle Sankt Bartholomä am Königssee
The pilgrimage Chapel of St. Bartholomew on the Königsee

Die Watzmann-Gruppe in den Berchtesgadener Alpen
The Watzmann peaks in the Berchtesgarten Alps

Der Rappensee nahe Oberstdorf
The Rappensee, a lake near Oberstdorf

Steinlingalm am Fuß der Kampenwand
Steinlingalm at the foot of the Kampenwand

Kampenwand, Gleitschirmflieger
Paragliding on the Kampenwand

Blick auf die Karwendelspitze
The peak of the Karwendel

Ausblick auf den Gipfel der Zugspitze
The Zugspitz's peak

Georg Kürzinger

Georg Kürzinger wurde 1957 in Oberaudorf geboren. Er studierte Informationstechnik und wissenschaftliche Fotografie. Nach seiner Diplomarbeit über Informationsverarbeitung beim menschlichen Sehvorgang arbeitete er in einer Forschungsgruppe zum Thema „Das Sehen des Menschen" mit. Parallel dazu begann er ein Studium von Kunstgeschichte und Ethnologie.

1990 wechselte er von der Theorie des Sehens zur Praxis und ist seitdem freischaffend tätig. Er fotografiert Reportagen, Bildbände und eigene Projekte, darunter „Ferne Heimat Kirgisien", „Das Ägypten des Nagib Machfus", „Heiligen-Parade" u.a., die in zahlreichen Ausstellungen im In- und Ausland gezeigt werden.

Kürzingers Fotografien sind geprägt von der Begegnung mit dem Fremden und der dadurch angeregten Neubetrachtung des Eigenen. So gelingt es ihm immer wieder, auch Deutschland mit anderen Augen zu sehen.

Weitere Informationen: www.gkuerzinger.de

Georg Kürzinger was born in Oberaudorf in 1957. He studied information technology and scientific photography. After completing his graduation dissertation dealing with information processing in human visual perception, he worked in a research group investigating the subject of 'human vision.' At the same time, he began studying art history and ethnology.

In 1990, he turned his back on the theory of visual perception in favor of its practical application, and he has been a freelance photographer ever since. He takes photographs for reportage features, photography books and his own projects, such as *Ferne Heimat Kirgisien* ('Distant Home Kirghizia'), *Das Ägypten des Nagib Machfus* ('The Egypt of Naguib Mahfouz') and *Heiligen-Parade* ('Saints Parade'), which have been shown in numerous exhibitions both in Germany and abroad.

Kürzinger's photographs are characterized by the encounter with the strange and unexpected, and the re-examination of the self that this gives rise to. In this way, he constantly succeeds in seeing his surroundings, and Germany, as if with new eyes.

For more information: www.gkuerzinger.de

Impressum

Fotografie:
Georg Kürzinger

Text:
Dominik Wichmann

Englische Übersetzung:
Andrew Cowin

Gestaltung und Satz:
komplus GmbH, Heidelberg
www.komplus.de

Gesamtherstellung:
Edition Braus Berlin Heidelberg GmbH

ISBN 978-3-89466-302-5

www.editionbraus.de